11-25-17

This Day Today

This Day Today

Inspiring Poems from the Heart

Doris Washington

To order additional copies of this book, contact:
Xlibris
1-888-795-4274
www.Xlibris.com
Orders@Xlibris.com
753843

Contents

Beyond The Sunset

As A Flower Blooms – Hope Lives

Morning

Beyond The Clouds

Peace

Possibilities

This Day Today

Closing Poem

Dedication

I dedicate this book to my devoted and loving husband, John.
And to my son John, who is my joy, and my inspiration to write.
Your love and support has made this work all possible.

Acknowledgements

I would like to give a wonderful thank you to my devoted and loving husband, John, my son John, the joy in my life, my beautiful mother, Emma Buchanan, my brothers and sisters, my dear friends, Barbara Roopnariane, Afi Heywood, Reverend Barbara Walker, Rhonda Dickason, Priscilla Gallegos, Eric Jackson. And I would like to thank those many wonderful friends support through the years of my poetry and writings. I would like to thank my dear friend Joni Meyers, whose support of my poetry, has encouraged me to keep going. And I would like to give thanks to all these beautiful people in my life who believes in me. Your love and support has made this work all possible.

Foreword

This Day Today are poems that touch the heart with hope, faith, inspiration and love. Each poem in this collection, inspires you to live each day full of promise, and to always find the joy in every moment of life. In the poem *As a Flower Blooms- Hope Lives,* I express to always hold on to hope no matter the challenges in life. In my poem *Beyond the Sunset,* I express that with *hope* we can come to love one another. And to know that *Love* is the answer to all things. Also in this collection, I dedicate two poems to Autism Awareness, *The Child That Plays Alone* and *Could You Sing a Song for Them?* As a mother of a son who has autism, my hope is to bring a better understanding to seeing the joyful side to looking at autism. Also, included in this collection, is a poem *A Flower for You,* that I wrote in honor of my mother, Emma Buchanan, whose love I cherish and hold dear. There also other new poems that I have written in this collection, that include: *Beyond the Clouds,* and *Direction,* poems that express the message about the search for *inner peace* we all seek and long for. And in the poem *Sunrise,* I express how to live each moment blessed and never giving up on your passion and zest for life. Also in this collection, I have included more familiar poems such as: *You, The Beauty of Love, I Wish to Live Life and Morning,* and a variety of new and familiar poems that I have written. We always have a choice how we live life, whether we find inner peace, whether we hold on to the blessings, whether we practice the act of faith, or whether we strive to make a difference in a positive way. My thoughts to the message of living a most fulfilled life is this: *a most positive life - is a most fulfilled life.* More than ever through the course of our daily lives, we will always need words of inspiration, that encourages us to live each day fulfilled. May *This Day Today* encourage all those who read its words, be inspired to live each day more fulfilled, and to the find the *joy* in truly living *Life!*

This poem is in honor of my Mother Emma Buchanan, whose love is so dear.

A Flower For You

As I look across the way-
On this warm and most beautiful day-
I see your smile,
Your quietness,
Your beautiful spirt of grace.
I give this flower to you.

You give so much,
And you ask for so little.
I admire your many years of wisdom.
And your unconditional love I treasure.
I give this flower to you.

You are like a beautiful flower in full bloom.
Your love never grows old.
And no matter my childhood days
Until now you are always there.
I give this flower to you.

I am thankful for the love you so give.
For because of all you do-
I cherish your love so dear.
A Mother's Love-
The most beautiful of them all.
I Give This Flower to you.

Poems of Dedication
For Autism Awareness

The Child That Plays Alone

In Dedication to Autism Awareness

He talks to himself and no one hears what he says.
His activity seems strange and unusual to some.

If only they would see his gift, he could accomplish
More than you know.
If only someone would take the time to explore
What he has.

He could be a great musician, a great artist, a great dancer-
A great athlete.
He has many toys and he plays by himself.
The other children do not understand him.
They do not play with him.

He likes to do the same things other children do.
And yet he is shut out from the world.
He is different, but aren't we all different.

If only someone would play with him.
If only someone would see His Gift!
The Child That Plays Alone

Could You Sing A Song For Them?

In Dedication to Autism Awareness

They exist, and you pretend they are not here.
They too have families who love them,
And hold them dear.
Could You Sing A Song For Them?

It may seem as though they may not hear,
And they may walk away.
If you could take the time to know about them,
You may see they have something to say.
Could You Sing A Song For Them?

They may become over anxious at times
For no apparent reason.
They have a difficult time understanding
Change in routine.
Could You Sing A Song For Them?

And they may not be able to communicate
Like you and me.
They may not tend to one task for too long.
For this is their Disability.
Could You Sing A Song For Them?

Their Disability is- Autism, Asperger's Syndrome,
Autism Spectrum Disorder.
And there are other terms too.
Could you give them a chance?
For they live here just like me and you.
Could You Sing A Song For Them?

Beyond The Sunset

As we hold on to hope for brighter tomorrows,
we can hold on to *Love*. Let's embrace love no matter
what we're going through- no matter what storms that
are upon us. For only love is our true salvation.
And more than ever, let's believe in its promise.
For *Love* we can come to know- *Beyond the Sunset*.

May We Come To Love

On this beautiful day so new-
Let us come to love.

May we look back to understand
That yesterday's sorrows
Can be today's triumphs of joy.

May we embrace our differences
With the understanding –
We are connected to one another.
And as we look inside our hearts –
To do what is right.

May We Come to – Love!
To know it has always been the answer.
For with Love we have Hope -
For a more beautiful world-
We know we can have.
May We Come to Love!

The Way of Love

As we hope for a brighter tomorrow.
May we see that even when the sun
Does not always shine each day as we awake,
That we can find- *Love*.

And may each of us discover
That Love is always inside our hearts
Ready to shine, no matter what each day so brings.

For love is not measured by how much wealth
Or material value one may possess.
But more so by the love one gives from the heart open wide.

As we hope for a brighter tomorrow.
May His Peace surround us always.
And may we come to know only
His Grace-
His –
Way of Love.

Always With Your Heart

Life has its challenges.
And there'll always be mistakes
We will make- even with the best of intentions.
But what's most important is that
You always answer to your heart.

Forgiveness is not always
About forgiving others,
But it's also about forgiving oneself.

Know that every step you take towards
Being your better self-
For every step you take for Him-
His Mercy! -
His Love! -
Will always be there for you.
He will give you *Favor.*

Life has its challenges.
And there'll always be mistakes
We will make- even with the best of intentions.
But as you answer always with your heart-
His Love will forever shine in you-
Always With Your Heart!

The Beauty Of Love

As you love, you live fulfilled.
And as you give love, you encourage
Others to give too.
But remember, there're times when love
May not be accepted or received by some.
And sometimes you may feel if it's worth the try.
But just stop and think
As you turn a negative situation
To a positive one.
You'll find much peace, much joy
You can ever imagine when you always
Answer to your heart.
Can you ever imagine anything greater?
For that's-
The Beauty of Love.

Love

It's everywhere.
It solves every problem.
It resolves conflict.
It makes a way for every solution.
It doesn't discriminate or judge.
It brings people together.
We can't live without it.
We may turn away from it.
We may cover it over with things.
And sometimes we may not see it
When it comes.
But-
If we step back, we can see it so clear.
We can see it through the smiles and the hugs.
We can see it through encouragement.
We can see it through a listening ear.
We can see it through the support of a friend,
Especially when we need it the most.
We can see it through patience, and understanding.
We can see it through kindness, and compassion.
Yes!- We can see it.
It's Everywhere.
It's-
Love

Hold On To Love

What brings us more together is- *Love*.
We can have many things to make our lives
Most comfortable.
We can climb the highest plateau-
Fulfill our dreams-
Give all that we own.

But what's most everlasting and more greater
Than we can ever have-
Is Love.

With *Love* we can always have hope
That each day will be brighter than yesterday.

And what we have now at this moment with *Love*-
We can live our dreams-
Give the best of ourselves-
And encourage others to know – *Love*.

Hold on to *Love!*
And let the *Love* shine inside of you.
Never doubt it.

For what brings us more together-
What's most everlasting-
More greater than we can ever have-
Is Love!

A Time, A Season, And Always Love

I pray more than ever now,
At a time where perceptions,
And what's on the surface
Has more weight, I pray for Love.

I pray for a revaluation of thoughts
To see love, and believe in it so.

For each season,
Each winter as the snow falls,
Each spring as the flowers blossom,
And the trees grow,
Each summer as more sunny
And warm days appear,
Each fall as the leaves fall,
And the cool winds fill the air,
I pray for each time,
Each season for love to stay.

I pray for a time where the act of trust,
And faith in humankind becomes more present,
Especially now.

I pray for Love to stay always,
Yes! Always!
I Pray for-
A Time, A Season, And Always Love.

Each Day I Awake

The world is most beautiful
When the sun shines on a-
Snow- capped winter's morning.

The world is most beautiful
When spring is in full bloom-
Trees of Cherry Blossoms,
And gardens of flowers all around.

The world is most beautiful
When summer nights showcase the stars above-
No matter where you are.

The world is most beautiful
When autumn leaves keep falling
On those cool days, just before winter.

And the world is most beautiful -
Each day I awake -
I still see *Love* no matter
Where I may be-
I see *Love* –
With the hope for an even brighter tomorrow-
Each Day I Awake.

Beyond The Sunset

As I look beyond the beautiful skies-
Before the night begins to fall-
I hold on to hope for brighter tomorrows.

Where hope lies-
I believe we can hold on to love.
For hope invites us to know- Love!

Love! is our true salvation.
Love will never fail us-
Only encourages us to see its beauty-
To give the best of ourselves-
To always answer to our hearts.

Love will always be there
For each of us to embrace.
And as we come to love
One another –
To believe in its promise.
Love! we can come to know-
Beyond the Sunset.

As A Flower
Blooms – Hope Lives

There will be days of rain that may never seem to end.
And all of sudden the sun will shine. As we have each morning,
as we awake each day, each time the sun rises, each time
a flower blooms, there's always *Hope* to hold on to.
With *Hope* and always *Faith*- we can know the joy in
every precious moment. And as we believe in His Promise-
we will see a blessing through every storm. For His Mercy -
His Love is always and forevermore.

Favor

He has you where you are for a reason.
And life is forever changing.
But without *faith*- things will remain the same.

Always move forward in- *faith*.
He can move mountains in your life.
He can carry you when you cannot carry on.
He'll bring the sunshine through the storms.

His Favor is your *faith in* Him.
Always be thankful for each and every blessing
He so brings.
And believe that what may seem impossible-
Is possible-
For every step you take in-
Faith!

Through and Beyond the Storm

See the sun as the storm comes.
He brings hope through it all.
Hold on to it always.
Trust in Him.
He's always there.
Sometimes life can bring
Many challenges.
Sometimes all at once.
And whatever comes to be,
Know it will pass.
Hold on,
And Pray.
For as the Storm comes,
Know He'll always be there-
Through and Beyond!

Hope

Giving up is surrender to no place.
When all seems lost, holding on
Brings you one step closer to the promise.
And as you believe each day is a new day,
Your trials can be your triumph.
Just believe that it all gets better,
No matter your circumstance,
No matter what you go through.
Believe what is now can change tomorrow.
Believe with Faith.
And always hold on to-
Hope.

3

In Due Season

When I think about all the blessings
He brings.
When I think about His Grace-
His Love -
I can only stay where He wants me to be.
I cannot doubt Him,
No matter what,
No matter the challenges.
And when the storms come,
And it seems as though they will not pass,
I look up to Him to know
He's my help,
He's my friend.
And whatever my desires,
I know He will grant.
Yes,
Always-
In Due Season

Always With Hope

In Dedication to the Survivors of Breast Cancer

Always with hope there's the reassurance
Things will get better.
And no matter what you're going through
At the moment,
No matter what trials you may endure-
It too will pass.

Always with hope you're encouraged
To never stop believing,
You're encouraged to hold on
To the blessings, He brings to you
On any given day.

Always with Hope-
There's the reassurance
Things will get better-
Always with Hope.

Believe what is now can change tomorrow.
Believe with faith, and always hold on to- Hope.

The Joy In The Morning

Life has its storms.
And there's always the joy in the morning
That can carry you through the night,
And the next day after that.
When problems arise,
And there seems no relief.
Hold on to the joy.
Let the sun shine through.
Believe it all takes care of itself,
No matter the storm.
And you'll find peace.
For Life has its storms.
And there's always –
The Joy in the Morning!

God's Peace

When the world seems too much to bear-
Too much to grasp-
I seek Your Peace within.
I find Your Strength to sustain me at all times.
And I pray more than ever before.
For it's Your Peace that flows like
The water along any brook or stream.
It's Your Peace that makes the new fallen snow
So beautiful on a brisk winter's morning.
It's Your Peace when the birds sing so lovely
On a warm summer's day.
It's Your Peace when the leaves fall
So gently in October.
It's Your Peace so beautiful.
When the world seems too much to bear-
Too much to grasp-
I look up to know You're always there.
With You-
Such Peace-
I Find.

May Each Day Lord I See You

Lord! -
May each day I see only You when trouble comes.
May each day I see only You when it seems no hope.
May each day I see only You
When the world is not at its best.
May each day I see only You
When sorrow is all around.

May each day I see Your Goodness
And Grace shine throughout
As the morning comes,
As the noon day appears,
And as the evening makes its way
Before I lay down to sleep.

And Dear Lord! -
May Your Peace spread through every
River, ocean, mountain, hilltop,
And every shore -
For all to see and know.
Dear Lord! -
May Each Day I See You!

As A Flower Blooms – Hope Lives

There's always *Hope* to hold on to.
And each time the rain comes-
The sun will shine even more brighter.

Sometimes life may throw us a curve.
All of a sudden it may seem difficult
To grasp.
But with hope and always faith-
We can know *joy* in every precious moment.

For as we have each morning-
As we awake each day –
Each time the sun rises –
Each time a flower blooms-
There's always *Hope* to hold on to.
For-
As A Flower Blooms – Hope Lives.

Morning

As the sun rises each morning- always be thankful
for another day. For every day that you have is a blessing.
Life is so precious. Each moment counts.
And for each day that you have, you have a chance
to do all that you wish for - hope for. You have a chance
to change things for the better. For each day is new-
each time the sun rises- each morning so new.

Sunrise

As the sun rises each morning so new.
I Thank God for another day.
For on this day I choose to live each moment
Even better than the day before.
And right now- I have a chance to do all that
I hope for- dream for.

Life is so precious.
Each moment counts.
And what's more beautiful for each day I awake-
I can change things always for the better.
Whether it's to make things right with someone-
Or whether it's to fulfill my true passion in life-
Each time the sun rises-
Each Morning So New.

Avenues

Alone I walk in the morning sun,
I find there're many roads to venture to.
Not sure where I'm going,
For there're many directions
To follow through.

With so much before me,
I find things can change
From one minute to the next.
And I'm learning life
Is all about passing the test.

I ask the Lord to be my teacher.
I ask the Lord to be my guide.
And no matter what my life may be-
I feel His Love inside.

Alone I walk in the morning sun,
I find there're many roads to venture to.
Not sure where I'm going,
For there're many directions
To follow through.
There Are Many-
Avenues

New

Each day is New.
Days passed are preparations
For what's ahead.
Each day you can always
Start over.
And as you awake, you have
A chance to do what you
Did not do before.
You have a chance to change
It all around.
For it starts with one person.
And as one does it, it can
Encourage others to do the same.
Just think about it.
For each day is-
New

Clouds For Today

The clouds tell us where we're going,
And the rain which is constant relays
So much.
Will the sun come-
Oh Yes!
It will tomorrow.
Spring doesn't seem like spring
At this moment.
The seasons will change a bit.
For all this has been foretold.
But will the sun shine.
Oh Yes! -
It will tomorrow.
Know this will pass.
Yes, it will.
The clouds don't have to cloud
Our hearts.
And the rain doesn't have to
Make us blue.
Remember the sun can shine,
Even when you don't see it.
The sun can shine in- *you!*
For right now, there are just-
Clouds for Today.

As Tomorrow Comes

Hope may seem difficult to hold on to.
And whatever challenges you may
Experience at the present day,
Know it's a temporary thing.
For today may not be your tomorrow.

Hold on to the *Hope* when it seems
Difficult to do so.
Just Hold On.
And believe the sun will rise again.
Yes! -
The sun will rise-
As Tomorrow Comes.

The Morning Sun

Revelations came to me
At the break of dawn.
Realizing many things.
Looking over my life,
How it has been,
Where I am now,
And where I am going.
Letting go of issues from others,
Issues I have, I'm facing
What I can't change.
And I'm moving forward to a new change.
My healing begins.
And I can see clear,
As I see-
The Morning Sun

A New Day Begins

Life is always changing-
And a new day begins.
Life has its challenges,
Its joys.
The good news is while
You're here there's always
The opportunity to live
Each day as if it's your last.
Take each experience
And always see the blessing
Behind every one.
Sometimes things don't always
Work out as we hope.
But never give up on *Hope.*
Sometimes the rain comes
To make room for the sun to shine
Even brighter.
For life is always changing-
And-
A New Day Begins!

A Christmas Prayer

As His Light shines, all over the world-
Pray for love everywhere.
As His Mercy- His Grace showers us so gently,
Pray for *Lo*ve in every heart.
As His Hand reaches out to us in sorrow and despair,
Pray our hearts will be open to His Vengeance-
Not our own.
As His Mercy comforts us when we need it the most,
Pray for strength and endurance
As He sees us through the storms.
As His Wonderful Love blesses us with the joy
In the morning,
Pray we always remember His Goodness
At all times.
As His Peace reassures us of His Everlasting Love-
Pray for His Love for all times.
For as His Light forever shines all over the world-
Pray for Love everywhere.
Pray! -
We keep *Christmas* always in our hearts.

Morning

Yesterday has come and gone.
Tomorrow brings promise,
And always hope.
And for now,
I'm doing alright.
Yes! - I'm doing just fine.
And each breath I take,
It's Good.
Yes! - It's All Good!
Hello-
Morning!

Beyond The Clouds

Always see the blessings He brings to you in every moment
of the day. For as you look beyond the clouds, find peace within,
and feel your heart with love.
For with a positive way of living, you'll begin to see that *Life*
is more beautiful and fulfilled this way-
as you look *Beyond the Clouds.*

The Beauty Of Life

Sometimes there are moments
Through life's journey things just happen
With no explanation.
And I have found that when I truly let go –
To come to peace –
Life is so beautiful.

For when things are not going so well-
And when it seems as if all is falling apart-
I find only when I let go of those things
I cannot change- I come to peace.

At this moment, I come to peace.
For no matter, what I go through.
No matter the joys and the trials-
I come to peace.
And more than ever I find-
Life is So Beautiful.

You

Silence after the storm,
The storm that was raging
So long.
The *Storm* is over now.
Time to start a new direction.
Time to find a new sense of purpose.
Leaving what is familiar,
Even with new ventures to seek.
The old will not be again.
And taking it one step at a time,
It will be alright.
For I'm here,
Alive like I have never been before.
Thank you, Lord!
I begin here!-
I begin with-
You!

Direction

Yesterday I cannot change,
But today I can.
And as I awake on this new morning-
I start again.

Mistakes are sometimes made
More often than not.
And I choose not to dwell on what is past.
But right now, I have a choice to live a better way.

Inner peace I so invite to have at all times.
I lean on Him always for guidance- for strength-
Each and every day.

Yesterday I cannot change,
But today I can.
And this choice to live a most positive life-
Is a *direction* I seek more and more.

Letting Go

Cleansing in one's soul.
Peace,
And serenity flows.
Hurt,
And pain released.
Your heart at peace.
Love steps in,
As you surrender it to Him.
Letting Go!

A New Day

I awake from a long sleep,
Yes, a long sleep from loneliness,
Self pity,
And regret.
I no longer choose to taste the bitter tongue
Of the trials of life.

I no longer allow worry, self-doubt,
And negative energy to be the focus of existence.
I no longer starve for others approval,
Opinions and love.

Forgiveness is what I practice.
Patience has become my daily routine.
Love keeps me alive.
And I seek Him always.
As I Start-
A New Day

New Life

As I move towards a new way of thinking-
Positive- leaving all old habits
Of negativity behind me.

I discover new oceans with a sense of direction.
Going forward I can plainly see.

The Sunset - the Blue Skies-
Oh, how beautiful it is to see God's creation.
For life is so precious
To waste even a minute
Of its treasures to go by.

As I stop and take time to smell the Roses-
I have a smile on my face-
With love in my heart for others-
For this I must try.
In knowing I can always begin again.
In an effort towards being the best I can be.
To seek salvation-
To live a better way.

And as I find I have complete serenity
Within my heart-
For then I can say-
This is a wonderful-
New Life

Beyond The Clouds

As the day awakes-
I move forward to discover
There's always a *blessing*
To encourage me to look-
Beyond the clouds.

Peace within my soul-
I seek more than ever now-
In a vast and ever changing world-
Where negativity abounds.

I feel my heart with love.
And with a positive way of living-
I can see the blessings He gives to me
In every moment of the day.
And I see that life is more beautiful-
More fulfilled this way.
As I look –
Beyond The Clouds.

Peace

Sometimes forgiving can be difficult, especially when feeling
hurt and disappointed. Sometimes even when the world is unkind,
being right doesn't hold too much. Letting go can be such a wonderful
feeling. To see a new day always starts with you. To understand what
you cannot change with no hesitation,
for the simple reason to be at peace.
As you let go of things you cannot change, and always be opened
to see any situation differently in a positive way, you will be able to
see the blessings around you. And inner
peace you'll truly come to know.

So Beautiful The River Each Time It Flows

The river is so beautiful each time it flows.
And on this day, I seek You more.
There's a peace that I so find-
As the waters of the river flows so calm- so serene.

All is well.
And when the challenges come,
I seek You more than ever in this quiet place
Where the river flows.
I hold on to hope that tomorrow will be better.
For today is a test of my faith.

Things do not stay the same.
Each day is new.
And there's always a blessing You bring
Each day in one's life.

On this day, I seek You more.
I Hold On.
I Hold on to- You!

Oh! How beautiful the river-
Each Time It Flows.

Time Heals, And So, Does Love

Time heals all wounds,
And so, does *Love.*
Time gives us a better perspective,
A chance to see things differently.
For that can only be *Love.*

Always forgiveness releases
The hurt, the pain before.
For one's life doesn't always stay the same.
Things can change in minutes, hours, and years.
The good news is, there's always a chance
To change things each day of your life.

Yes, time heals all wounds.
But it's always the choices we make.
For as we invite the love to come within,
As we start to see the goodness in everyone.
We'll find that time not only heals-
And So, Does Love.

Always There

You're always there though every trial,
Every triumph,
Your peace I find.
I lift my head up high,
Knowing my help comes from-
You.

I Praise You,
Every minute,
Every hour,
Every day.
For You're always there
Guiding me through it all.
Reassuring me so much.

You're my salvation,
My joy in the morning
To hold me as the evening comes,
And on to the next new day.

There's so much I can say about You.
Your Goodness,
Your Grace.
And I Thank You
To Know-
You're-
Always There.

The Lord Watches Over Me

I do not fear the darkness at night.
For the sparrow stays within my sight.
Oh! How the Lord Watches Over Me.

I do not fear the arrows that come at me
During the day.
For the Lord is all around,
He is with me in every way.
The Lord Watches Over Me.

I do not dwell too long in despair.
For I know I am in the Lord's Care.
The Lord He Watches Over Me.

I trust in the Lord, I hold on to His
Unchanging Hand.
For when I am weak, He helps me stand.
The Lord Watches Over Me.

I will stay in the house of the Lord,
He will never leave me.
For I know with faith,
He is with me through eternity.
Oh! How the Lord Watches Over Me.

The Armor of God

Only by faith I go forward.
For all things are possible with God.
And through the storms
He's always there.

He gives me favor to know-
That no weapon formed against me
Shall prevail.
No weapon formed against me
Will take my – *Joy.*
No weapon formed against me
Will devour my – *Faith.*
No weapon formed against me
Will destroy my – *Hope.*
No weapon formed against me
Will not keep me from *Praising Him!*

Yes! All things are possible
With God!
For He gives me Favor! -
And with the blessings He so brings-
Through every trial – through every- *Joy!*
Only by *Faith* I go forward.

A Daily Prayer Poem

Dear Lord I Pray-
You give me strength for each day.
Guide me when I'm lost.
Hold my hand when I'm afraid.
Heal me from the hurt and the pain.
Help me let go of things I cannot change.
Anoint my spirit to always do what is right.
Teach me - show me Your Way.
Dear Lord-
This I Pray!

May Peace Be With You

As the morning breaks on this most beautiful day-
I rest my heart with no heavy sorrow.
Only such wonderful thoughts I hold dear of you.
And with every joyous moment while you were here-
I hold on to the understanding it was your time to go.

Each day I find peace.
I cherish the times no matter how brief.
I am blessed with the joy you brought –
And much more.

Sometimes we may not understand why
Those we love cannot stay?
But as we cherish what they have given
To us- whether it be inspiration or – Joy! –
We can find peace.

And as each day passes –
As we remember the beauty of what
They brought to our lives-
As we remember them-
May Peace Be with You.

Home

Balancing it all together,
What makes sense is the
Purpose of why I'm here.
Where I am meant to be-
At peace, always,
In my soul, always.
And yes,
Love, I find everywhere.
While other things come, and go,
Love never dies!
I see the morning sun,
I start a new day.
And it's all because of You.
You have given me new life.
More Greater than I can ever imagine.
It never left me.
Though at times I've moved away from it.
And this is where I will stay.
So, glad I found my way back- here.
Dear Lord!-
So, glad I'm-
Home.

Peace

Sometimes forgiving can be difficult,
Especially when feeling hurt and disappointed.
Sometimes even when the world is unkind,
Being right doesn't hold too much.
Letting go can be such a wonderful feeling,
And the world will seem much nicer.
It's a matter of perspective.
It's a matter how to deal with it
In your mind- in your heart- in your soul.
To let go with no hesitation for the simple
Reason to be at-
Peace.

Possibilities

When you truly believe in you, encourage yourself to
never give up. And no matter what obstacles along the way,
you can overcome. When it seems, your dreams are beyond
your reach, keep believing in possibilities.
Always believe in the deepest desires of your heart.
For as you move forward always in faith, believe everything
is possible. Live your dreams. For what seems impossible,
is possible when you believe in you.

Words of Encouragement

I awake this day encouraged.
To know I can do all things possible with You.
For I cannot go back to where I was.
Nor can I stay where I am.
But as I move forward-
I hold on to the promise.

Your blessings never cease.
And Your Enduring Promise is the reassurance
There's nothing You can't do.

I can rise above any storm imaginable.
I can overcome any obstacle.
My faith is renewed.
And more than ever before I trust in- You!
I Awake Each Day-
Encouraged!

The Love Inside Of You

Take the disappointments
And make them your blessings.
Always stay positive no matter
What each day brings.

For it's all up to you.
You always have a choice
To live a full or half full life.

Rise above what you cannot change.
And focus on what you can.
For yesterday is past,
And today is a new day.

There's always a blessing through
Every experience.
And with each experience –
There's always something you can learn.

Live each day as if it's your last.
Press forward with faith.
And most importantly –
Always Keep-
The Love Inside of You.

The Leap of Faith

Take the leap of *faith* and believe
Each step you take empowers you
To go the distance.
Find strength through each challenge
You so endure.
And when disappointments come,
Receive them as blessings
To keep going even more.
Never give up,
No matter what comes your way,
No matter how difficult the climb.
Just know as you keep going,
His Mercy,
His Love,
Will never fail you.
Take the Leap of Faith -
And *–Believe.*

Disappointments

Sometimes no matter how much you try,
No matter the heart's sincerity,
They come unexpected like a flood in
Your heart of disbelief.

Sometimes the cost can be so severe,
And you may find it hard to understand.
Sometimes dreams can be deferred
With many obstacles and barriers to overcome.

Forgiving those who let you down brings peace.
And forgiving self allows you to move on.
Today does not have to be your tomorrow.
Blessings come even when things are at its worst.

Keeping the door open *to hope- to promise-*
Can make a way for dreams fulfilled.
And with your *faith* to believe in it so.
No matter the-
Disappointments

Foundation

Rebuilding- starting over
With dreams set in motion,
There's a life to get back.
Reorganizing and going another direction,
There's a feeling this time it will be different,
This time it will be better.
And as one storm has passed,
Then before you know comes another one.
But this time it's different.
And as the peace within you overflows,
Prosperity is not far off.
Rebuilding –starting over
With dreams set in motion,
There's a life to get back.
My Life!

Obstacles

You can't change yesterday,
You can change today.
And tomorrow there'll always be *Hope*.
There'll be bridges to cross.
There'll be storms to get through.
And those obstacles will come when you least expect.
The good news is-
As you keep going, and believing,
You can do anything you set your heart to do.
With the Faith,
Your dreams can surface at any time.
Just Keep Going!
Just Keep Believing!

The Most Beautiful Gift

Life itself is a blessing.
And there'll be disappointments
Along the way.

And for every –
Challenge you so endure-
Find the joy and peace within.

Hold on to every blessing-
And begin to love you.
Follow your passion-
No matter where it takes you.

For each day you have begins
With you and how you live life.
And the most beautiful gift
Is the *Love* you give each
And every time you breathe – *Life!*

Winners

Winners see beyond the boundaries,
Always searching high.
Winners always say: "I can do it"
Believing their dreams can come true.
Winners never quit.
They stay the distance all through the end.
Winners don't compare themselves to others.
Only strive for the best in themselves.
Winners live by courage, and faith,
Standing tall with a job well done.
Winners see beyond the boundaries,
Always searching high.
Shining beautiful like a Star!

Possibilities

Hold on to your dreams
For the possibility to come true.
Never stop believing-
For a *Blessing,* may come to you.
And if you find your dreams you reach for -
Seem impossible to achieve.
Continue to hold on to your dreams-
And Believe.
Hold on to-
Possibilities

This Day Today

This day I begin a new- found journey- full of the promise
and the faith that I have found with You!
For You have given me new life.
This day I stay always encouraged, to focus on the
goodness of others, to stay positive in any given situation.
For each day, I awake- I pray to always work towards being
a better person, practicing the act of forgiveness, making patience
my daily routine, and always going with love in my heart.
Thank You, Lord! I begin here! I begin with- You! -
This Day Today!

The Beauty Of You

As you come to love who you are-
All you can give-
The beauty of you will shine even more.

Only you can define the gift
That is yours alone.
And when you begin to see the inner you-
Having the faith in all you can be.
You can rise above any challenge imaginable.

As you come to love who you are-
As you embrace your own uniqueness-
You will always give the best of who you are.
And the beauty of you will always-
Shine Through!

I Have A Song In My Heart

I hear the birds Sing.
I receive the Lord's Blessing.
Oh! How beautiful the Sound.
God's presence is all around.

I sing no sad song.
Unhappiness does not last long.
With such joyful tears,
I've learned through the years.

Life is precious and worth living.
The best of me I keep giving.
I trust in God always.
Peace,
Joy,
And Love I carry with me
The rest of my days.
For-
I Have a Song in My Heart!

I Wish To Live Life

I want to receive the Lord's Blessings every day.
I want to be at my best,
Even if I'm at my worst in every way.

I want to hold on to only good feelings in my heart.
I want to move on from disappointments
As I make a new start.

I want to be receptive of change and not lose me.
I want to always in every situation,
Open my eyes and see.

I want to look back at the past to reflect,
And not feel sorrow.
I want to hold on to hope
As I look forward to tomorrow.

I want to always to *"keep the faith"*
For dreams to come true.
I want to not remain sad, lonely, and blue.

I want to always let positive thinking
In my life play a vital part.
And-
I want to always have *Love* in my heart.
For-
I Wish to Live Life!

Start Anew

When you start anew,
Just remember to keep you.
For each situation, you journey is different.
And each one you meet is not the same.
Go into each experience leaving issues
Of the heart behind.
Let positive thoughts fill your mind.
Forgive, even if it's hard to do.
And just let Love take you,
When you-
Start Anew

I Cannot Stay Where I Am

This change I find in me,
Empowers me to never give up.
To endure,
With Faith.
And whatever obstacles along the way,
I can overcome.
Today I own this for self,
And go forward with a new vision
To know all things, I dream for,
Hope for,
I can achieve.
I cannot stay where I am.
And I Thank You Lord for This.

His Amazing Love

My Lord! -
You're my strength- my song.
You're the joy in the morning –
My healer of all my hurts- my pains-
You're my salvation.

For no matter what I go through.
For no matter what each day may bring-
You keep blessing me through it all.

My Lord!
You not only heal-
You're merciful-
And Yes! -
You're a fixer too!

For to trust in You I must.
With all my heart and soul-
I surrender it all.

My Lord! -
You're my strength- my song.
You're the joy in the morning-
My healer of all my hurts- my pains-
You're my salvation!
You keep blessing me through it all.
Oh! Your Amazing Love!

Praising You

I Praise You during the storm,
And after the storm has passed.
I Praise You when it seems no relief,
And for each blessing You bring.

I Praise You when the river overflows,
And when the sea is calm.
I Praise You when the world is not at peace,
And when peace is all around.

I Praise You when the rain seems to never end,
And when the sun shines so bright on a given day.

I Praise You for my trials,
And for the strength You give me each day.
I Praise You for prayers answered before,
And after.

I Praise You for letting me know
You're always there,
And for being my friend.

I Praise You for Your Guidance,
And for the reassurance that You bring.

I Praise You for the challenges, and
For that anchor, as You see me through.

I Praise You for reminding me what You're
All about, and for teaching me so much.
I Praise You for each and every day,
And for loving me as I am.
Dear Lord!
I cannot stop-
Praising You!

Thank You For This Day

Dear Lord-
I Thank You for this day.
This day as I begin a new-found journey.
Full of the promise and the faith I have found
With You.
I Thank You for each blessing You bestow upon me.
I sing with abounding joy of Your Love.
And as I awake each day,
I ask for Your Anointing –
Giving me the reassurance
That with-
Your Grace,
Your Mercy,
I can always begin again.
Dear Lord-
I Thank You for This Day.

Fulfillment

There are those moments we may find-
We're not where we should be.
The good news is-
As you work towards what you can change,
Always in you, such peace you'll find.
For to walk with Him only gets better
Each day you breathe life.
And as you leave behind
The old life you once knew,
Welcoming the new life,
Nourishing your soul
With His Love,
Lifts you up evermore.
The blessings overflow,
Encouraging you to continue the journey
He has in place for you.
Always to be-
Fulfilled.

This Day Today

This day today,
I took a moment to breathe,
To laugh,
And to smile.

This day today,
I saw hope through the disappointments.
To stay always encouraged.

This day today,
I focused on the goodness.
To know all gets better if one believes.

This day today,
I practiced the act of Faith,
To keep going,
To never give up.

This day today,
I took a moment to breathe,
To laugh,
To smile,
And to Pray!
This Day Today!

Closing Poem

This Poem I dedicate to my son John, my joy, my inspiration to write.

My Inspiration

Your smile- I wait for each day.
You are the joy that keeps me going.
And on every wake of each morning-
I'm thankful to God for you.

You teach me so much.
To love the beauty of you.
To love you as you are.
And most importantly
All that you give to me.

I love your uniqueness.
And whether if the day seems cloudy or not-
You bring the sunshine.
You are my inspiration.
I wait each day for – your smile.

CPSIA information can be obtained
at www.ICGtesting.com
Printed in the USA
BVOW03s1922231017

498441BV00001B/12/P